The Cry of My Heart

A collection of poems written during a time of great pain, living through a divorce, and self-reflection, finding my strength in Christ when I didn't have the strength to go on

KRIS BERTOLINI

ISBN 979-8-88851-958-5 (Paperback)
ISBN 979-8-88851-959-2 (Digital)

Covenant Books
11661 Hwy 707
Murrells Inlet, SC 29576
www.covenantbooks.com

THE AFFAIR

The darkest of black takes over my mind
The pain and the shame I feel all the time
I gave my heart to the man I love
It was precious and should have been treated gently like a dove
But instead, with one hard squish against my will
It was beaten, battered, and bruised during the kill
The kill of my heart that leaves me alone in the night
With almost no desire to even try to fight
To step into the light and out of the shame
My fear is that I would have to do the same
Break his heart and leave him alone in the dark

How Can I

How can I see the beautiful colors in a world that has become so gray
How can I be devoted to my one true God when my desires led me
    astray
How can I encourage others to do the things I cannot
Like be so grateful for the things I got
How can I feel joy when depression threatens my life
How can I let go of this world and its daily strife
How can I live one day at a time, when worry of the future are
the chains that bind
How can I find balance when I'm weighted down by sin
How can I let all this go and begin again
How can I call on Jesus's name, when I can only speak
through my shame
How can I accept this free gift of grace when most days I can barely
    look at my face
How do I live a simple life when my brain is so complex
How can I plan for the future when I don't know what comes next
How can I make friends when I don't like myself
How can I like who I am when I dream of being someone else
I don't know the answers, and I don't understand
But I know the Holy Spirit living in me can
So I will just continue to move and seek His face
And I will walk one step at a time to the lighted place
The place where my dependence on me doesn't matter
That place where all I've known has been shattered
That place where grace is given by love, a love that can only
be from heaven above

COURAGE

I'm standing alone in the darkest of night
I close my eyes as I shudder with fright
I can feel the demon's cold breath on my face
I pray so hard for God to take me from this place
I open my eyes to see where I am
I find myself looking straight at him
The demon was there with nothing but a smile
He says, "I guess your God has left you for a while"
I know in my heart that cannot be true
As I cry and scream, "God, where are You"
The demon just laughs and says, "I won"
My reply to him is, "This battle's just begun
You cannot have me like you did before"
I will not stand here crying anymore
My God has not left me, He's my power and my strength
To Him in everything, even you, I give thanks
Yes, I'm afraid but I will not run
I will stay and claim the victory my God has won!

DAYDREAM

✛✛✛✛✛✛✛✛✛✛✛✛✛

How can I live my life when all I'm doing is dreaming
It makes me happy, but it has no meaning
How can I let it go when my life hurts so bad
Living in my dreams takes away all the sad
I can be someone else and do anything I please
I can go anywhere, anywhere my mind sees
I can be perfect and gorgeous and have any man love me
And all night long, he will kiss and hug me
I have friends who don't betray my heart
In my dreams, I have a fresh new start
I know dreaming isn't the only way
When I close my eyes, I should start to pray
Change is scary when you're all alone
But I know You are with me, so I know I'm not on my own

RAGE

The redness of rage takes over my mind
When I close my eyes, I see the devil every time
He's so terrifying, it's hard to see his face
I open my eyes as if to run from that place
That place of a haunting consumption of anger and hate
A place if I give in for only a moment evil would be my dying fate
I drop to my knees and pray with my heart
That Jesus and I will never ever part
I know it's my choice, my own free will
And that's the part that scares me still
Fear is the evil that surrounds my day
I know in Jesus, there is another way
Another way to live and be free
I want so much for that to be me
I will stand strong in my fear and make Satan hear
"You cannot have me" are the words that I say
My Jesus is my life, my truth, and my way

Lord, Please Help Me

I feel like I'm floating in the sea lost and alone
Not knowing which way is home
Lord, please shine Your light so radiant and bright
Reach out Your hand for me, save me from my drowning sea
Breathe Your breath of life upon my face
And let my life be in some new place
Away from the anger and tears that have filled my heart for so many
    years
You came and gave Your life for me
And I want it to be all it can be
To serve You, and praise You, to give my life to You
I want people to see me
And see who You created me to be
Wrap Your arms around me tight and hold me with all Your might
Save me, Lord, from the devil himself
Who torments me with shame and guilt
It seems everywhere I look, he's there
I close my eyes and pretend not to care
But he knows the truth and so do You
I'm afraid to look because it might be true
I know I need to open my eyes and stand strong in my faith
Because the only way to leave is to walk out of this place
And to follow Your light that leads the way, to my new life that I can
    have today

GUILT

✤✤✤✤✤✤✤✤✤✤✤✤✤

Guilt is something I have lived with for years
Guilt has caused me to lose many tears
Guilt is something that gets into my mind
And torments me daily, it is not kind
Guilt is the heavy load I carry with me down the road
Guilt is that somehow my existence itself
Has caused pain and grief to everyone else
Guilt is a lie that's easy to believe
Guilt is the one thing that keeps me from being free
I hate guilt and want it to go away
So that I can begin to live my life today

THE NEW ME

My life is changing before my eyes
I no longer wake up and count the days until I die
I now understand the peace in God's grace
And I know my life is no race
I look to my future with a smile on my face
And I know I'll have joy in that place
That place of unknown that God is leading me to
Knowing with my whole heart I can do what He asks me to
Everything I want is just moments away
And I know without a doubt that I'm okay
The Lord is my strength, it's amazing to me
I had to lean on Him for it to truly be
He was there holding me gently in His hand
Knowing not one more day of this pain could I stand
Why did it take me so long to really trust
To find true joy relying on God is a must
I am a new creation in Christ today
And I lay my life down for Him in every way
I love the Lord with all my heart
I know that He and I will never part

CHURCH

What is a church, I hear it all the time
Does anyone have an answer that doesn't end with making it mine
What is a church if it's not exciting and fun
It's lots of work that needs to be done
What is a church, a country club open only on Sunday
Or a place to forget about when you wake up on Monday
What is a church, a place to be loved for who you are
A place to love others for who they are
What is a church, is it a part of who you are with every heartbeat
Is it the very thing that makes you complete
What is a church, no one really knows
Because the answer is different everywhere you go
What is a church, we ask it so many times
But really the answer is not hard to find
What is a church, *stop* for a moment and ask God in prayer
And in that moment of quiet, He will lead you there

FINALLY FREE

It's so nice to finally be free, to live my life and just be me
I love You, Lord, I want to lift my hands up and shout
So that everyone knows without a doubt
That You are the light that they see in me
And that I am everything You created me to be
I can see the world through Your eyes
I have to tell You, it's quite a surprise
I look at people and see the beauty You see
And I love them, Lord, the way You love me
I can feel Your peace flowing from my heart
Hand in hand we walk, knowing we will never part
I never thought feeling like this could be real
I thought sadness was all I would ever feel
All it took was a three-letter word, *yes*
And my life is no longer a mess
With a snap of Your finger, You changed my heart
And Your heavenly kingdom I am now apart
I will love You forever and serve You all my days
I will give You glory in many, many ways
I am excited to see what kind of life You have for me
I know I will love it, whatever it may be!

DAD

Who is this man that I call dad
For my life, he's the only one I've had
But I don't know him and that makes me sad
And I never will because his health is very bad
He's going to die and I don't know what to say
So I just sit by his bed and on my iPod I press play
I want to wrap my arms around him so bad
That's not the relationship we've ever had
So I just sit here with my headphones on
Just listening to song after song after song
His distance is not because he was mean to me
It's just the way it had to be
I never saw him again after that day
I never said what I wanted to say
I didn't tell him I love him or I'll miss him
I just left filled with regret and grim
Even now I don't know what to say
So I've never visited his grave
It's been a decade, and I still feel lost
I didn't know what my silence would cost

RAPE

Why is it the cold of one dark night
Can leave you shivering with terror and fright
The sin of one man so dirty and cold
Can leave a stain on your life that's as sickening as black mold
I can feel his touch in the look on any man's face
And the fear on that day makes my heart begin to race
My wall is shrinking pound by pound, and a beautiful woman inside
    is found
To live with the fear of what happened yesterday
There is no room for it in my life in any way
Yes, what happened was horrible, it's true
But to let it go and move on is what I must do
The question is how because I don't know
But I will struggle and fight to make it so
I will walk with God's hand in hand
When it becomes too much, He will carry me through the sand
I trust You, God, to keep me safe and to take away the fear of that place
I see the beauty of the rainbow ahead, and I will trade my fear for
    that instead
Because with God's strength on my side, I no longer need a place to hide
I will knock my walls down and stand in His power
And give all the glory to Him in that hour
I am a strong woman that He has created
Not a pitiful woman that the devil has berated
This fear will control my life no more
My wings are spread, and with God, I will soar

STRESS

There are so many thoughts running through my mind
The voice just talks and talks all the time
It says the same thing and does not stop
My mind is spinning like a toy top
One moment of peace that's all I ask
Then you can get back to your mind-boggling task
Of driving me crazy in my own skin, as I continue to play a game I
    won't win
What does it mean really to "let it go"
Does anyone ever do that, I don't think so
But it comes in moments, *gifts* here and there
I had one yesterday and with you, I'd like to share
The peace I found in the presence of sleep
Warmed my heart and allowed me to feel every beat
I could feel the rhythm dancing in my soul
And a calmness of mind began to take hold
I could feel my anxiety just drift away
And I knew I was in the presence of the Lord today
I could see the peace on your beautiful face
As I watched you dream of some faraway place
Knowing that your mind is at rest is for me what makes this moment
    the best
You gave me your calmness and sense of peace
Yesterday in that moment when you allowed yourself to sleep
Thank you is what I'm trying to say
Because gifts don't always come in the most obvious way
"I should have been better" is what that voice will say
Tell it to shut up and send it on its way
We never know when God will use it in some great way
He used you for my moment of peace yesterday

A Good Day

For years, I have walked up the steep mountain side
Carrying a load so big I thought my soul had died
I have struggled and fought with every ounce that I had
Thinking when I make it to the top, I'll be glad
So I walked and walked with that glimmer of hope
Determined that no matter what happened, with it I could cope
I take a deep breath as I stand at the top
And realize my struggling and fighting can stop
As I stand up so high and see all the glory
I see now it's only the beginning of my story
I see all that God has to offer me
I see everything He has created me to be
I can see the power and might in the palm of His hand
I'm so overwhelmed that I can barely stand
Fear and excitement are swimming around inside
But not the same fear that makes me run and hide
I'm not sure which step to take from here
Because everything I see, I cherish and hold dear
I just want to sit for a moment in one spot…
And breathe in the glory because I made it to the top!

Alone

The pain I feel in my body runs so deep
All I desire is to lay myself down and weep
It starts at my feet and goes all the way up to my head
It's hard for me to process anything that is said
Because the pain gets in and takes over my mind
And to me, of all the pain that's the worst kind
It starts in my mind and goes to my heart
And slowly word by word just rips it apart
This is the moment when I need so much
To feel loving arms and a tender touch
They are not there is what my mind will say
And then with my heart, it begins to play
I've been alone for so many years
And I have cried and cried so many tears
I'm not quite sure what's harder to bare
Being alone or with a man who doesn't care
Either way my heart's still sad and dreams of something it's never had
Why is it easy for me to give love away, yet I long for it every day
Why is my heart not hard inside
I would think it should be from all the tears I've cried
And the games my mind plays surely have taken their toll
But I guess it's because it's never seeped into my soul
But still the desire of my one true love
Is something that in my heart is often thought of
When will it be, soon, soon, soon I pray
Then with my hopes and dreams, I awake for another day
I know that God has a great love for me ahead
And waiting for that day is not something I dread
I guess what I feel that makes me so sad
Is that it's something I've never had
To be someone who's full of so much love and tries to take the high
    road above

It baffles my mind and confuses my heart
Why for so long I've lived in the presence of the dark
I just thank You, God, for keeping me safe
And preparing for me a much better place
Although I go slowly the anticipation is great
Because I know what's ahead, and I just can't wait

FULLY RELY ON GOD

This is the song of my heart that sings out to You, O, God
You have grown me into a beautiful flower, but I began as a tiny pod
You knew who I was before my time began
Never for a moment did I leave the safety of Your hand
I have traveled the road of trials in many different ways
But I was always saved by Your amazing grace
Every tear that ran slowly down my cheek
With your love and faithfulness I was given another peak
My stem grew strong, and my petals became soft
Because my weeds and dead branches You lovingly cut off
My heart overflows with the most amazing love
One that as only a human I could never know of
You remain beautiful and true until the end
And this message to the world I will send
I love You, Lord, with all my might
Thank You for leading me by Your light

GOODBYE

✛✛✛✛✛✛✛✛✛✛✛

What do you do when you wake up one day, and your dream is gone
Where do you find the joy and strength to go on
How do you let go of something you wanted so bad
When all it leaves behind is a broken heart that's gloomy and sad
I pray for God to let me walk away with grace
And the courage to see the reality that I must face
I won't go so far as to say the last years have been a lie
But my haunting thoughts wonder if your friendship I did buy
I wanted so much for your feelings to be true
I would spend hours dreaming of you
Even if only to have you as my friend
Gladly with you an eternity I would spend
I feel you don't want me, and I must say goodbye
And that is why my heart is sad and I cry
You always had time for me when I had money
And now that I don't, you're busy, and that's what strikes me as funny
There is no anger or hate that I feel for you
My desires and intention for you are true
I must let go and give you the freedom to walk away
But my prayer of course is that with me you will stay
If that's not the road that our lives will take
Never for a minute will I think it's all a mistake
You gave me a strength that I needed to go on
And the love that I felt made my heart grow strong
I pray your life will be abundantly blessed
That for you, God will provide nothing but the best
So do not spend one moment worrying about me
God will use this for His glory and bless me abundantly
I know your heart was not evil in its intent
I know you enjoyed the time together that we spent
You will always have a special place in my heart
Even if the dreams of us are ripped apart

I love you is all that I have left to say
God will give me the strength if you choose to walk away
I miss you already as my heart says goodbye
But I can feel the strength of not living a lie
The day will come when my dream comes true
Only time will tell if it will be with you

MY BUTTERFLY

I can feel the fresh air as my wings break free
But I'm standing in the middle of who I was and who I will be
I dream of the day when I'll spread my wings and flutter away
The joy of waking up and knowing today is the day
The day I begin the "out with the old" and "on with the new"
Knowing exactly what Christ put me here to do
Sometimes I wonder if that day will come at all
I fear as I struggle to break free of my cocoon with let loose and fall
Fall to the ground with one fatal splash
Leaving behind dreams that are broken and mashed
How hard should I fight because I don't know
I don't want my worst fears to be so
I grab hold of my faith and hold on tight
I don't move at all as I shiver with fright
Relax…are the words my God says to me
Take a deep breath, and just let this be
My hand is quick, and I will catch you if you fall
Not one dream break, I will protect them all
Feel the beauty of who you are, and you can flutter as high as the stars
I know it's hard being stuck in between
Living your nightmare and wanting your dream
Just be patient, My precious butterfly
You've never left My watchful eye
I want you to fight so you can feel the freedom of breaking free
Don't give up because you're doing it to glorify Me
I am your God, and I love you, My dear
Seeing your beauty in My eye brings a tear
I'm sorry your cocoon is a dark and lonely place
My heart aches because it's taken the smile off your sweet face
When it becomes too hard, My hand will set you free
And I will raise you up with My strength for all to see

You are stronger than what binds you in that cocoon
You will break free, I promise it will be soon
You will have all the desires you dream
And My radiant joy from your face will beam
Thank You, God, for these words You say
I will hold on to them every single day
I can feel Your strength, my spirit is renewed
Now I know exactly what I must do
I will rise up in Your power and fight with Your strength
And for everything that happens, I will joyfully give You thanks
You are my God, and for You, I will fight
Because I know in the end, it will be alright! Amen.
(2 Corinthians 5:17)

FORGIVE US, FATHER

As I sit here and look at the people around me
I can't help but wonder how their lives must be
Little girls skipping while their hair bounces back and forth
Grandparents beaming with smiles of course
But then there are those whose eyes look like mine
And I wonder do they want to cry most of the time
What is it about life that makes us all so sad
Some say its desire for things never had
I'm not sure that's what I believe
I think too many of us get what we please
I feel like I live in a world I don't belong
Because all that's important to me I'm told is wrong
They say what's important is how much money comes in
They are the *rich*, and it's said with a smirkish grin
I say what matters is how your money goes out
That's how you know what a person is really about
I watch you drive along in your *fancy* car
Honking at everyone because you feel like you're a star
You think you're better than the person on your right
Polluting our world with your emotions wound so tight
What's wrong with our world, that question's not tough
Our focus and desire is to accumulate more and more stuff
To make things change there is one thing we must do
We must remember that God said, "Love others as I have loved you"
God is soft and gentle and His love is true
And that's the love we should give too
But instead of loving others to the point of sacrifice
You want what you want to the point of strife
You allow anger and greed to consume your heart
You are the people tearing our world apart
The things that you have, none of it matters
And your wallet can grow fatter and fatter

The sadness I feel is for all of you because you fulfill the
statement, forgive them, Father, for they know not what they do
I wish there was a way that I could make you see
Your selfish behavior is causing so many tragedies
You're not number one, quit thinking that you are
Let others around you shine like a star
The joys you seek can only be found one way
Take what you have and give it away
Whether it's money or time or the shirt off your back
Give it away with no strings attached
If everyone would start seeing the world with their heart
People would no longer walk around ripped and torn apart

A Moment in Time

As the sunlight breaks to begin a new day
He slowly opens his eyes but has nothing to say
He sits up first, then puts one foot on the floor
Another day to remind him he has no one to wake up with any more
He walks into the other room and lets out a sigh
His lonely heart breaks, and a tear rolls down from his eye
He goes into the kitchen to get something to eat
He sits quietly at the table remembering times that were sweet
Hours pass by, and he has yet to utter a word
He thinks talking to himself is completely absurd
He looks at his watch, and a smile takes over his face
He will see his friend soon, he knows the time and place
He cleans up his mess and gets himself dressed
He is filled with excitement and wants to look his best
He gets in his car and drives the right way
In his mind, he thinks of the clever things he will say
He walks through the door and is only halfway in
When he sees his friend standing there with his welcoming grin
"How are you today?" is the start of their talk
He pays for his drink and continues to balk
Telling him stories and showing off his wit
This continues for a moment then the old man turns to sit
He sits there as smiles as he watches his friend
Who is smiling and chatting with new customers coming in
For this moment in time, he is completely thrilled
Because at this moment, his heart has been filled
The day winds down, and the young man locks up
Thankful that the chaos for today has finally stopped
He grabs his keys and heads out the door
Not knowing the purpose of his life anymore
He has a life time still ahead to live
But he's feeling downhearted like he has nothing to give

The success of this world and all its lies
Makes him feel like a failure not matter how hard he tries
The sad thing is that when his day will end
He will never know to so many he's been a faithful friend
He'll never know the hearts he's filled or the lives he's touched
He will never know to so many he means so much
Success in life is not measured by a dollar bill
Success in life is measured by the hearts we fill
That's the purpose that God gave us all
No matter where in life we may find His call
So when you wake up each day put your smile on
And know that through you many lives will be touched upon

Save Me

My Lord, I cry out and ask You to save me
I'm drowning in my sorrow, and I can no longer see
The shadow of darkness is not far behind
It's desperately trying to devour my mind
I'm running so fast that I'm losing my way
And I don't know how I can wake up to another day
Another day of sadness is what I wake up to
Another day of praying "Lord, what do I do"
When will it end, when will my mind be free
When will these demons quite tormenting me
Sometimes I think that day will never come
I think the demons tormenting me is their fun
You promised me, Lord, You would always be near
But Your voice is so soft, I can't tell if You're here
I close my eyes and quiet my mind
In the stillness, You say if I look, I will find
But all I see is darkness, and I want to run and hide
Somehow I know You're right by my side
Holding my hand and guiding me through
I don't have to think, You know what to do
I'll hold Your hand, and You lead the way
And together we will claim Your victory over this day

ANOTHER LONELY NIGHT

Oh, Father, I'm drowning in the sadness of my heart
I'm begging You, Lord, for my new life to start
The loneliness I feel devours me like a lion
And my mind is lost in the tears that I'm crying
I try so hard to wait and be good
Doing all the things that I know I should
But where are the arms You will use to hold me tight
Where is the heart You will use to love me through the night
I have longed for love all my days
And I have looked for love in all the wrong ways
But here I am, Lord, I stand before You now
I drop to my knees, and in Your presence, I bow
Here I am broken and as empty as can be
Fill me and love me, with You, Lord, I plea
I can't stand one more day of doing life alone
I need someone to be there when I come home
I give You this burden that I can no longer carry
Only You know the man You'll send for me to marry
Until that day I pray that You will keep him well
And that You will keep me from the torment and hell
Of this bondage that I'm in because it's crushing my soul
I'm crawling on my knees as it's taking its toll
Take it, Lord, I give it all to You
Take it all because You know what to do
As I sit here crying, I reach for Your hand
Please pick me up and set me on Your rock to stand
Dry my tears like You've done before
And please let me feel this pain no more

FAREWELL

I really want to please You, Lord, and use this gift to reach the world
But I don't only want to write of dark times that are bad
Or how many tears I cry because my heart was sad
I want to write of Your beauty and grace
And Your mighty hand that spreads from earth to outer space
I want to stand on the mountain top and shout "*I love you*"
And say "yes Lord I'll follow, just tell me what to do"
I want to look at everyone deep in their eyes
And tell them, "Don't you know Satan is filling you with lies"
Can't you feel the love of the breath that brought you life
You don't have to live in Satan's world and bow down to his strife
I want you to be free of all the lies
The lies that daily over and over Satan tries
You're not good enough, why would they listen to you
You're too weak to do anything God has called you to do
The words are like ping-pong going back and forth in my thoughts
He did it again, he spun his web, and I'm caught
I can hear you laughing and mocking me in the back of my mind
Your sarcasm so sweet, pretending to be kind
You think you have me, that I'll never be free
But God's salvation is a gift, a gift He gave to me
So go ahead and laugh your way through the day
Pack your bags and be on your merry way
I don't care about the lies you tell
I know longer bow down and submit to your hell
I will shout that I love the Lord
I will fight you with His righteous sword
He will always be more powerful than you
And He will give me the strength to do everything He calls me to
You are really only a pathetic angel that has fallen
And since that day you have been on your belly crawling

You still don't get it… You can't win
Oh, that thought to my face brings a grin
You are no longer a dark cloud hovering over my day
And never again do I have to listen to the lies you say
I know I have the choice, and that's the cross I carry
And that will be with me until I die, and my body they bury
But from this moment on, I will never be afraid to say
That I love my Lord in every way
I will reach the world and tell of His great love
Because that's what true disciples are made of
So farewell, Satan, the tables have turned
Because the bridge to my mind I just set on fire and burned!

GIGGLES

Oh, Lord, I can feel Your joy filling up my soul
The dark cloud has lifted, and it's no longer taking its toll
I close my eyes, and I can see Your light dancing inside of me
I'm savoring this moment of peace because I'm free
I can see the girl inside me just skipping about
Just letting out a little giggle not feeling a need to shout
How wonderful it is walking hand in hand
This day is so crystal clear that we take a moment to sit on the sand
I sit and listen as you tell me of all the great things yet to be
And for the first time in my life, I can look across the sky and see
See the greatness of who You are
I can see one finger on earth and another on a star
You are more beautiful than I ever imagined you to be
And the peace in Your eyes is burning right through me
I can feel Your Spirit strengthening every weakness I've ever had
I can feel Your finger fill the holes in my heart that were made when
    I was sad
I can feel the wholeness beginning in my toes
As it fills my body it's driving out all my woes
It's amazing to me that time as short as a breath
Is how long it took for You to put my demons to rest
It seems like a lifetime ago
I was praying for this moment to be so
I can hardly wait for all Your dreams for me to come true
I will love every one of them, no matter what You'll have me do
Thank You, Lord, for letting me feel the love of Your hug
I will end this day now as I climb into bed snug as a bug
The warmth of Your love will get me through the night
And peacefully I'll sleep because everything is alright

GOD'S HANDS

As the sun rises up to take its place in the sky
The Lord scans the earth with His watchful eye
He is taking in the sight of His children below
As He's telling His angels where He wants them to go
He opens His hands and releases His glory
As the angels fly to fulfill His story
There was one angel with God's special request
"My son is in need and must be saved quicker than the rest
I love him so much," were the words the Lord said
"And seeing him in pain one more day I can no longer stand
Oh, he is special, and I have blessed him so
But you must hurry, he's lost and doesn't know which way to go"
The angel was soaring to earth at light speed
Because the Lord's child was in desperate need
It didn't take long before she was by his side
And when he looked into her eyes, he knew he could no longer hide
She reached out her hand and gave him a smile
And told him, "God has sent me to walk with you for a while"
He reached up and grabbed her hand
And she quickly pulled him out of the sinking sand
God used her hands to heal his heart
Because the pain that he's suffered has ripped him apart
The beauty she sees in this man God created
Has left her heart overwhelmingly elated
It's amazing the lies Satan has made him believe
They have held him down and kept him from being free
Each touch of her hand takes his sadness away
And he grows stronger and stronger with each passing day
"The doors are all open, I'll help lead the way"
Are the loving words his angel did say

"Look to the light, and see all its glory
God has a very special chapter for you in his story
So close your eyes, and don't make a sound
And fear not, my love, an angel can never fly too close to the ground"

DARKNESS

Where are You, Lord, I cannot feel you beating in my heart
The blackness of sin is ripping You and me apart
I'm all alone, and I feel nothing but hate
As I stand and ring the doorbell of hells gate
Go ahead and open I don't really care
It's the shame of my own sin that's brought me here
I know you're here, Lord, in my darkest hour
And I know You can save me by Your strength and power
But I feel so ashamed, I want to run away and hide
I feel like I deserve all the darkness I feel inside
You gave me a gift that would bless me every day
I was so thoughtless that I threw it away
I'm so sorry that I didn't have more strength
I'm so sorry that I didn't wake up every day and give You thanks
Please give me a chance to make it right
Please let my actions be honorable in Your sight
I love You so much, and I can't bear to be apart
I don't want to exist if You're not the beating of my heart
Please draw me close into Your presence once more
And fill me with Your joy so I will overflow like before
Forgive me, Father, for my sin
Please let me feel Your love again

I'm Safe

I love You, Lord, with every ounce of my heart
You have Your hand on me, and Satan can never tear us apart
He tries so hard with his crafty ways
Twisting and turning things until they seem okay
But no matter what happens, You will only let me go down the road
    so far
You're always there to grab my hand and guide me back by Your star
Even when I feel ashamed and alone
Your arms are always wide open to welcome me home
I love the moment when I snuggle in tight
When You hold me and rock me, I know everything is alright

HOLD ME TIGHT

In my Daddy's arms is where I long to be
To feel You holding and gently caressing me
You make all my troubles go away with Your hug
You hold me so gently and yet so snug
Nothing can hurt me, I'm safe in Your arms
Satan can't woo me with his trickery and charms
I want to stay here for the rest of my life
And never again deal with any pain or strife
Hold me tight, Jesus, and never let me go
Hold me tight, and let all my dreams be so

REFRESHED

Breathe Your breath of life into me once more
Give me Your power so with eagle's wings I can soar
You are the beauty that's in every moment of my day
I will shout it out from the mountaintop in every possible way
My love for You, Jesus, is bursting out of my heart
I praise You, God, for giving me a fresh start
Every day is made fresh and new
I devote every one of them to You

MY GOD IS

My God is the tenderness in every drop of dew that hits the flower
    petal
As it slowly rolls down to the middle as it settles
My God is the power of the thunder as it roars
And the strength of a lightning bolt as across the sky it soars
My God is the mercy of every storm that stops just in time
And turns it into a breeze so we can hear the music of the wind chime
My God is the grace of the sun as it rises each new day
And the light that guides our path along the way
My God is the love of all the beauty that our souls take in
From the very moment, we're born and our lives begin
My God is amazing in every single way
In more ways than my human brain could possibly say

I LOVE YOU

Thank You, Lord, my heart overflows with praise
With gratitude in my heart, my hands to You I will raise
As the words from my lips sing out to You a song
I will say I love You, Lord, all day long
Your breath of life You have breathed into me once more
And with Your power, I will begin to soar
There is no mountain too high or valley too low
For Your love and mercy will always overflow
You love me, Lord, with amazing grace
And I want to give the world a taste of who You are
So come live in me and shine Your light for the world to see

DISGUST

I hate myself, that's how I feel
There is nothing good about me that's real
I'm always the one who wants and never gets
I'm always the one filled with regrets
The pain in my heart runs so deep
I cry all the time, and I can't sleep
I look in the mirror and hate what I see
It's my reflection looking straight at me
I yell at myself so I'm filled with more shame
I willingly accept my criticism and blame
You're stupid and disgusting, and no one wants you
I've heard it since I was a child, so it must be true
Lies are truths in the ears of a child
Whether they are spoken loud or mild
How do you move forward when you're confused
How do you repair a heart that's bruised
I don't have the answers, it's true
But with God's grace, I don't have to
With Him, I can walk broken with tears running down my face
And I don't have to hide because this is a safe place
His words are kind, even if they are hard to believe
It soothes my soul, and my mind is relieved
Maybe someday I can believe them without doubt
Maybe someday I'll know what love is really about
I know the road from here to there is long
I do believe You will make right all that's wrong
Thank You for baring my shame on the cross
And for saving my soul so I'm no longer lost

MANKIND

My heart cries out for you, O, God
My soul aches, and my mind is in a fog
I need Your hand to touch upon my face
And stir within me that special place
That place where love and contentment I will find
That place where all my chains You will unbind
It's so easy to get lost in the world these days
The quest for self is available in so many ways
How did our world become so lost
That we would forget what Your bloodshed cost
You came and died for a love that's so great
You have taken the burden no matter how heavy the weight
I see the beauty in Your journey to the steeple
You took the time to stop and love the people
I ask for that gift so that I might share
The peace of Your love because I do care
But the gift has really been given to me
Because the beauty of Your people I do see
It has nothing to do with money or houses
With fancy cars or designer blouses
It's not about who we know or where we've been
It's not about what church we've been
Or what church we begin
It's not about our wants, our desire, or our needs
It's not about being generous or living in greed
It's that part of You that every soul has
That one special touch that adds the pazazz
You have created each person with such beauty and grace
And I can see it in the smile of each beautiful face
You're a master of perfection, and yet we see it as a flaw
How many mornings I've looked in the mirror and imperfections I saw

How sad you must be, do Your eyes shed a tear
Because I can feel the pain as I draw near
To spread Your love use my heart
I'm only one person but that's a start
Use me as a light for all the see
The beauty in the person You created them to be
Help us all take the time to see
That I'm no greater than the person next to me
You came and died for the love of us all
You hold out Your mighty hand so none of us will fall
Help us all to love with Your heart
I know we're just human, but that's a start
The gift of love is the greatest of them all
So prepare your hearts because Jesus has come to call
He's called you to step up and say what you're about
He's called you to live your life inside out
So step out of the world and don't be afraid
The debt that you owe has already been paid
So I end this poem with one last prayer
One last gift that with you I will share
The answers you seek you will surely find
But only when you learn to love mankind

DADDY

I miss you, Daddy, and I want to come home
I long for Your touch, can You feel my soul moan
It's so hard to walk in this place
I miss seeing Your beautiful face
I want to be in the presence of Your light
Your radiant beam shines with such might
In Your presence, there's no pain to speak of
Only the power of Your mighty love
Here on earth among demons, I walk
I hear their lies all day as they talk
I miss the safety of Your big strong arms
Keeping me safe from Satan's charms
If I close my eyes, I can see You sitting there
As I climb up in your lap, You begin to stroke my hair
I breathe out my breath and breathe in Your peace
Our hearts are connected with a love that will never cease
I know You've sent me here to spread Your love
And to speak of things they could never dream of
I will honor You until You bring me home
And I know You have not sent me here to walk alone
Together we will walk hand in hand
And together any demon we can with stand
So even though You're there, and I'm here
We still have our love that's so dear
But nevertheless, I miss You so
But I carry You with me wherever I go

Light the Way

I'm sitting at your feet as a tear rolls down my eye
My anger has turned to sadness, and there is nothing left to do but cry
I ask that my soul will be refreshed like the morning after
You've watered the earth
Wash away any dark seed with in me and replace it with Your good-
    ness and worth
My desire Lord is to do Your will and share the beauty of Your heart
But Satan webs a trap in the shadow of my mind, and we are oceans
    apart
I'm drowning in the sea as I search for You, my body is limp as my
    head sinks down
Blackness is all that my eyes see, and I can feel evil all around
Your hand is strong enough to save me, Lord, and Your power can
    light the sea
Use Your army to slay these demons that seek to haunt and destroy me
Faith my, Lord, that's all I need to draw up Your mighty sword
To defeat these demons and receive all the blessings that for me You
    have stored
My eyes are focused, and I can see You now as I walk across the sea
Your arms are wide open as You stand on the shore waiting eagerly
    to receive me.

DESPAIR

I can feel myself slipping into the sea of despair
It's a familiar place, I've spent many years there
I need Your hand to hold me tight
Or I'll slip away into the dark night
One day has passed when I was full of so much love
The direction of my future I was sure of
But now I sit, and my eyes hurt from crying
Don't lose hope… I know, I'm trying
But the love I felt is slowly slipping away
I can feel it running through my fingers as every moment passes today
I always mess up, I can never get it right
Why do I try to do things on my own might
I'm sorry, Lord, that I'm such a mess
My chance has passed me by I guess
I want him to love me as more than a friend
But to have that now is only pretend
Because he doesn't look at me the same way
I can't go on thinking everything is okay
But maybe he's thinking that I feel this way
And he's hurting inside not knowing what to say
Help me, Lord, I'm lost in the sea of my mind
If I turn to You for answers, I know I'll find
So hear me, Lord, and answer my prayers
And give me the strength so my feelings I will share

WORSHIP

As I sit in my chair and look upon a man I don't know
I can see the most radiant and beautiful glow
As I watch him singing standing there with his hands raised
With such peace on his face, I can't help but gaze
As I look at this man, I can see his soul inside
Just loving his Lord with no fear to hide
This moment is rare, it's what true worships about
And I have been blessed by his peace without a doubt
I had to meet him, just a quick moment to say hi
As I shook his hand, I looked him in the eye
I could see the heart of Jesus like I've never seen before
And I could feel my Lord's presence deep within his core
There was nothing flashy or fake about this man
Only a deep understanding of God's divine plan
Love others as I have loved you
I can see with every last breath that's what this man will do
The love and care that he extended to me
Is a very big blessing from God you see
I have searched and prayed and waited a lifetime
To find someone who has the same heart as mine
Who will do anything for someone in need
And not even think… I've done a good deed
There is no gift that's greater than love
That is what our salvation is made of
To wake up every day with the eyes of the Lord
Is a prayer I've prayed many times before
I will continue to love with every last breath
Until God takes me home, and my soul is at rest

VISITATION

Silence is a valley very deep and wide
It's an empty hollow space with nowhere to hide
It's a torturous land where I'm trapped in my mind
Where the chains of depression I will surely find
As I stand in front of these chains on the ground
The smile that was once upon my face has fallen to a frown
I hate the fact that I'm all alone
That no one will walk through the door and say, "Honey, I'm home"
It's bad enough that my heart you betrayed
But through your visitation, you've taken my kids away
How do I live without my kids for ten days
My soul is restless, and my mind is crazed
This is the part of life I say is unfair
I didn't use drugs, I didn't have an affair
But here I am, forced to let my kids go
Surrounded by a society with the attitude "so"
Where are the days when you were killed for your sin
Stoned in the court never to be dealt with again
I know, a little harsh in my thinking, you say
But I just hate it so much when my kids are away
Okay, Lord, I give You this pain
I know by holding on to it I have nothing to gain
So now I'm back to being empty and alone
Eagerly waiting for my kids to come home
I guess I should give You the sadness of my heart
But there are so many pieces I don't know where to start
So, Lord, I give You this jumbled-up mess
Because only You know where the pieces fit best
My life is a puzzle, and only You see the picture on the box
I know I must be careful because Satan is a sly fox
So even in the midst of my sad, broken heart
You and I will still never part

So I guess I'm truly not alone
Because I just walked in Your door and said, "Daddy, I'm home"
My smile is back in its rightful place
And tears of joy roll down my face
I just needed to sit and put my head on Your chest
And let my heart find peace and rest
Just for a moment, a blip in time
Then I'll get back to the assignment that's mine
I know with Your strength all things are possible
And You and I together, Lord, we are unstoppable
So even though I paused and looked
In me, those chains did not get their hook
Thank You, God, for never leaving my side
And always giving me a safe place to hide

WHAT I SEE

When I look in the mirror, I don't see what you see
I see everything that's been said and done to me
I see all the words that my mother ever said
Memories come flooding in and the pain I dread
I see someone unworthy because I didn't pay my dues
I see a girl who use to be smart, what happened to you
I see the disgust that use to be on your face, but now it's on mine
While putting food in my face, saying words that are unkind
I see a teenage girl who is desperate for love
Willingly doing anything to be approved of
I see the terror of being raped in that house
I see the fear inside that makes me timid as a mouse
I see a reject that's not worthy of love
So far down my feelings I shove
They rise up and surface every now and again
But I swallow them back down, smile, and pretend
In order for me to truly be free
I must allow them to surface and let them be
Jesus says I'm worth so much more
But there is no room for these words to store
Just replace one old with one new
I think that's something I can do
Just one, are the words of my savior
Start with the truth, you are favored
And add to that how much I love you
I stepped down from heaven to be with you
I gave up my life on the cross
So that you no longer need to be lost
Take my hand and walk with Me
And let Me show you how life is supposed to be
Don't worry we can go as slow as you like
Just hold My hand with all your might

One day what you see will be in the past
And in love and joy, your soul will bask
I love you, I love you, I love you so much
Feel the healing in My touch
If you need to cry or scream, go ahead
It changes nothing that to you I've said
You want to be angry, I'm angry too
This is not the life I've dreamed for you
So let's change it into something great
And you will bring glory for My sake
Okay, Jesus, this one thing I know I can do
I know I'm safe when I walk with You
I want my life to bring You glory
So I will let You write the rest of my story

DOWNCAST

I'm sitting here with so much rage inside
Everything You've said to me is a lie
You don't answer the dreams of my heart
You sit by and watch as I'm being ripped apart
I hate You are the words I want to say
But I can't bring myself to truly feel that way
Please, God, tell me why
Why more tears I have to cry
Am I destined to just be alone
For my soul to be tortured and my heart to moan
This thing You call love, it isn't real
It's only pain that my heart can feel
I blame You, Lord, for every tear I've cried
And for all the hope I placed in Your lies
I don't think my soul has ever been this lost
I'm afraid of what this despair will cost
How strong must one person be
Why can't You just come down and save me
Why do You always build my hopes up so high
And then smash them until I want to die
You have the power to make things change
That's the part I find so strange
How can You look down upon my defeated spirit
And say, "If you pray, I will hear it"
I've tried so hard to honor You
I've loved others the way You've told me to
My soul is dying deep inside
I no longer have a place to run and hide
I don't have the strength to stand anymore
I can't even run into Your arms like before
Why have You left me alone here crying
With a heart so deflated I feel like dying

I'm too strong to let Satan beat me like this
He will not be adding me to his list
Okay, God, we both know I will not give in
I can no longer wallow in this self-pitying sin
So, Satan, you've really only given me more power
I can feel it growing stronger by the hour
I'll pick myself up and hold my head high
It doesn't matter how many tears I cry
I will always honor you, my Lord
And in battle, I will always draw Your sword
The very essence of my beating heart
Is the love You placed there from the start
Wash my soul, Lord, with the tears I've cried
Thank You for showing me that I don't need a place to hide
I am who I am, and that's good enough for me
Because it's exactly how You've created me to be

FRIENDSHIP

As I look deep into your eyes
I can see your soul inside
It's a place where so much beauty lives
And a heart that overflows with the love God gives
I see great compassion that you're trying to give
Struggling with that in the life you're trying to live
Feeling sometimes like you're the fool
People thinking your eyes are covered with wool
When you act in love don't ever doubt
Because that's what the true love of Christ is about
When God looks at your beautiful face
And sees the love you spread all over the place
It brings a tear of joy to His eye
Because it was with love, He sent his Son to die
I can feel the strength of the tears you've cried
I can see the depth of your soul inside
You have a peace in your spirit that soothes my heart
I have felt that joy from the very start
God wants you to know that He is pleased with you
Because you're a man that's honest and true
So on the days you rip yourself apart
Remember that God sees the beauty of your heart
I'm so glad God has allowed our paths to cross
If for no other reason than to remind you you're not lost
You are exactly where He needs you to be
Spreading His love for all to see
Don't think for a moment with your sharp edges I'll be cut
Just live by that feeling you have in your gut
I hope you'll be blessed by my love too
Seeing it's a gift that God's giving you
I hope one day I've proven to be your friend
Because I'll stand by your side until the end

IN THE VALLEY

Darkness has fallen across the valley sky
I know God has placed an angel nearby
But anger blinds me, and all I can see
Is Satan's army rising up against me
This is the part where I stand strong in God's might
But this time, I have no strength to fight
I feel lost and scared and alone
I don't know which way to walk to get back home
I cry, and I cry and fall to my knees
"Help me, Lord!" is my only plea
I try to hear that small voice in the cloud
But these demons are laughing at me so loud
They think they've won so they celebrate
They think my soul has become their fate
You foolish demons, go ahead and cheer
I may not hear Him, but I know my God is near
He is wondering this valley looking for His lost sheep
He will waste no time, not even to eat or sleep
He can feel every tear that falls from my eye
And He longs to hold me and wipe them dry
Why, Lord, do I feel this pain
Why through my tears does Your Kingdom gain
The answer to that question I already know
It's the only time I'm not busy and on the go
That's the moment when I draw you close
And allow You to love me the most
I'm going to sit and wait right here
Until You find me so You can draw me near
I love You, Lord, with all my heart
And my soul is Yours, each and every part

MY SHAME

✢✢✢✢✢✢✢✢✢✢✢✢✢✢

O, Lord, I stand before You, and my body is weak
The love in Your face is all I seek
My sins have caused the dark night to come
It's Satan's army from whom I run
I'm running fast toward Your light
And I'm holding on to You with all my might
Don't let me go for I fear I might fall
And never reach Your precious light at all
Who is this person that I've become
To my evil desire, I did succumb
Forgive me, Lord, for betraying You
Because I knew the right thing to do
Your mercy and grace bring tears to my eyes
Your love tells me You've heard all my cries
Protect me in the safety of Your arms
And help me resist all of Satan's charms
Use my shame for Your great glory
And save others from the pain of my story
Fix my eyes so I can only see You
And with Your wisdom, show me what to do
I love You, Lord, more than I can say
And I will tell You that every single day

MY SONG

Write a song or praise about the trails in my life, oh, where should I
      begin
Should I speak of the nights I cried so hard I prayed that it all would end
Or maybe the days I was consumed with anger and hate
And I knew for certain that hell would be my fate
Or all the times when everything just seemed to be wrong
And no matter how hard I tried in my heart, there was not a single
      song
I could speak of the loss that still pains my heart
But there would be so many I wouldn't know where to start
What I've been through doesn't matter because we have all been
      through the same
The only thing that matters is that you cry out Jesus's name, *Jesus...*
      His name so precious it washes peace over me
And when I think back to what He's done, I can't help but fall to my knees
With worship and praise and a song in my heart
Because He has been with me from the very start
Through every battle I've had to fight
He has stood in front of me like my shining knight
For every tear that I've ever cried
Jesus has always been right by my side
With His arms wrapped around me tight
Loving me with all His might
And every day I've wasted with anger and hate
Jesus reminds me, by the grace of God, hell is not my fate
The day that He stretched out his arms for me
Is the day that says, no matter what happens, with Him I'll spend
      eternity
Thank You, God, for giving up Your Son
And for being with me every moment since my life began
I love You more than my words could ever say
And I freely give my life to You every day!

HELP

Oh, Jesus, my heart is so lost within me
I'm crying out to You, hear my plea
I'm running from the pain that rips me apart
I try to sort it out, but I don't know where to start
Do I start with the tears that I'm afraid will never stop
Do I allow myself to burn with anger that literally makes my skin hot
I feel like I can't move on, like I'm trapped in these chains
That my heart will forever be broken by these pains
I want to move on, I want to be free
Please, Jesus, I'm begging You to help me

EYES OPEN

I can see the light of life that God has for me
I can feel the power of God and all that I will be
For the glory of God will be my light
With the power of God these demons I will fight
They cannot have me, not one more day
I will take God's hand, and He will lead the way
To the victory He has won on the cross
Now and forever God is my boss!

FREE

Hallelujah, I praise You, Lord
I have been spared from Your righteous sword
The blood of the Lamb has washed me clean
The sins I've committed will never be seen
I fall to my knees and lift my hands high
And my face is wet with tears I cry
There will never be enough words to express my love for You
But I'm going to spend the rest of my life trying too

I Need You Most

When I wake up each day,
I'm tired and dismayed
I long to feel Your touch upon my soul
My trials have taken their toll
I love You, Lord, with all my heart
But my sinful thoughts are ripping us apart
Wrap Your arms around me and hold me close
It's Your approval I need most
Yet I spend my days working so hard
Looking at the green grass in everyone else's yard
I don't understand why my heart wanders away
With every amazing blessing You give me every day
Search my heart and make me right
I'm so tired of this worthless fight
You're the only thing that matters, I know it's true
Help me keep my mind and heart focused on You

Trying to Make a Friend

It's so hard waiting to see if you're going to be my friend
My mind keeps spinning, it's driving me off the deep end
I want to scream and hug you and tell you I love you so much
And other times I wonder if my heart will flutter at your touch
I love the sound of your laugh and the expressions on your face
And the way I feel around you, it's like serenity fills the space
In my mind, we are already lifelong friends
Always there for each other till the very end
I want to call or text you, but I'm afraid I'll chase you away
But it's so hard to play it cool and wait for another day
The funny thing is I don't know how you feel
I know what you said, but I don't know if it's real
Maybe you feel the same way as me
But maybe you think I'm crazy and hope I'll go away
Hoping to avoid me each passing day
I know what I want and what I've prayed for
So I just need to wait to see if God opens a door
Either way, my thoughts and prayers will be with you
With extra-special blessings on whatever you choose to do
You already hold a place in my heart
Whether this is the end or a beautiful new start

It's Tough Being a Woman

It's tough being a woman in the world that we live
There is so much of ourselves that we give
If it's not the house, the kids, it's the PTA
There just aren't enough hours in the day
This world tells me that I've been set free
Stand up and fight and don't let anyone push around me
These chains are heavy in this freedom I've won
I run myself ragged trying to get everything done
Do I have the right clothes, is my makeup just right
How much do I weigh, I think I've gained a pound last night
Perfection is slipping so far away
But if I try a little harder, I might get closer today
It's tough being a woman, that's not true for me
When I get lost in this world I fall to my knee
I find myself wrapped in the arms of God's grace
I feel renewed as He gently strokes my face
He gently removes all the world's chains
And soothes away all the world's pains
My beautiful daughter, if you want to know who you are
Just ask me, I've created you to shine brighter than any star

5 YEARS OF HELL

I've been dead inside for so long
No love, no passion, no heart song
I've been walking around feeling so lost
Buried under the guilt that my sin has cost
I've betrayed You, the one I love most
How can I live my life, and in Your name, I boast
It's been five years that I've been locked in this cell
Five years of torment and hell
Blinded by the truth that You have forgiven me
That moment five years ago when I fell to my knees
Blinded by the truth that I'm covered with Your blood
That I've been unwilling to let go of all this crud
Living my life with my eyes focused on me
Trying to make myself into who I think I should be
I just can't do it anymore
I can't be the same person as before
I freely give you my heart, Lord
I will stand and fight with Your righteous sword
My eyes are fixed and locked on You
I will not run but do anything You ask me to
I love You so much that it frightens me
Because of the power, I can feel welling up within me
But I can finally let go and fall into Your embrace
And I can see the joy on Your beautiful face
Finally reunited, the way it should be
Finally together, You and me

DROWNING

I feel like someone punched a hole in my heart
Two hours ago, I was overjoyed at a new start
I felt excited, strengthened, and renewed
I could see clearly what I must do
Now I feel lonely and desperately sad
I feel like I lost all the joy I just had
I will not give into the darkness coming my way
I will fight with all my strength every day
I'm crying out for your help God
I feel I'll drown in my sorrows and sobs

Bright Morning Sun

I want to write something beautiful, but I'm filled with hate
I'm so lonely, and I fear this is my fate
To walk through life all alone
To never have someone waiting at home
Will anybody care if my life would end
At my funeral, would there even be one friend
No one cares in this stupid world I live
It doesn't matter that I give and give
The world is full of users and takers
Loves that are nothing but heartbreakers
It seems like to have a friend you have to be a bitch
Or throw around money because you're rich
It seems like if you're sweet and nice and show a little love
No one cares what you're made of
I don't understand, and I guess that's what's wrong
I let this confusion play my heart song
I don't want to feel this way anymore
But I don't want to fake my life like I did before
I want to learn to finally be free
Rid myself of these demons haunting me
But I can't, I don't have the strength to do it alone
And I don't have to, that's why Jesus left his home
He's already won this battle I face
And the Holy Spirit is forever pleading my case
This victory, this freedom I seek
It's already mine to forever keep
I don't have to stress or fight or worry
God has come to be with me in a hurry
I already feel peace and joy again
Just since this poem began
Thank You, Lord, for saving me
For answering as soon as You heard my plea

I love You forever, and with You, I'll always stand
Going through life together, never letting go of Your hand
The dark days don't matter with You by my side
I no longer feel the need to run and hide
I will walk down the path with the demons at my back
And no more will I fear they will attack
You are my shield, my protection, my strength
And for the joy You give me, I give You thanks
My life will never be lonely or sad
I can let go of all the hate I had
When Satan starts to play his game
I know I just need to call out Your name
You will rush to save me from torment and hell
You will grab my hand and save me from my dark lonely cell
You will love me and hug me and hold me through the night
You will remind me that everything will be alright
I know You have a beautiful life planned out for me
And I know exactly where I'm supposed to be
I trust You, Lord, with every breath of my life
I know I need to get my eyes off my sorrow and strife
I know I need to fix my eyes on You
And every day that's what I plan to do
You are the love of my life, You're all I need
With every bit of strength to You I heed
Whatever Your will, so it be done
From the darkest of night to the bright morning sun

I Love You So Much

I can feel Your presence in every breath I take
Every thought I have or decision I make
I love You more than my words can express
Whether I'm overflowing with joy or crying out in distress
You're the only one Lord that I need
You have loved me through every plea
I thank You for all the times You told me no
I thank You for giving me direction when I didn't know where to go
The dark days when I thought I needed a man
I look back and see one set of footprints in the sand
Here I thought I was all alone
And I see You were carrying me home
My journey has been long and hard
It's left me bloody with lots of scars
There isn't one thing I would change about it
Because of Your love for me, I'll never doubt it!
You were with me on the days I was betrayed the most
You were here with me when victory was claimed, and in Your name,
    I boast
My heart, I completely give to You
Do with me whatever You want to
I trust You, Lord, in every possible way
I devote myself to You every single day
You're all I want, You're all I need
And Your instructions daily I will heed
I embrace the freedom You freely give to me
I'll use it so I can be who You want me to be
Every part of me belongs to You
My love for You is deep and true

CAGED

I feel like a rat trapped in a cage
About to explode, full of rage
I feel like my life is living me
Everywhere heartache, cries, and pleas
Sometimes I feel like I finally broke free
I run so fast into another cage that's trapped me
The walls are different but the cage is the same
I don't know how to get out, how to win this game
Some days I struggle, it's just too much
I know I have to fight so I won't give up
I don't know the way to be free
Be who God made me to be
Stop trying to be who everyone wants me to be
Just be who God called me to be
It doesn't matter if I don't always know who that is
Because the plans, not mine, it's His
God knows better than I could for all these years
If I would listen, I would stop crying all these tears
I would have joy in my heart and peace in my mind
I would never again be trapped in these chains that bind
God is the only one who can lead me from the maze
He has the key that unlocks every cage
The freedom I seek will never come from approval of man
It will only come with my eyes fixed on Jesus as we walk hand in hand

ONE LIFE TO LIVE

Sometimes I feel like my life is over, I'm filled with so much sorrow
and regret
Heartaches filled with broken dreams, nightmares filled with sins I
can't forget
Forty-five years seems so young, so why do I feel so old
Probably because my search for love has been in a world that's bitter cold
It's ripped me apart from the inside out and left my bloody heart
lying in the street
It's not sorrow from one great love but sadly from everyone I meet
I've searched so long for a place to fit in for love, for family, for friends
And when it didn't work out, I picked myself up and tried again
But now I'm tired, and I feel like my life is over
It's done, I found no lucky clover!
I think of all the things I wished I'd done
I would gladly trade my rivers of tears for barrels of fun
I wish I would have danced instead of being afraid
And then looked back and cherish all the memories I made
I wish I would have hoped in the car and hit the open road
And reaped beautiful seeds I would have sowed
And kept going until I found a place to call home
But instead, I tried to please everyone else, I pleased no one, and I'm
all alone
That's the problem with not being who you truly are
It leaves you sad and lonely and unsatisfied
It leaves bitterness and regret for things never tried
So hear me now, take the advice I give
Don't be afraid to be who you are because you only have one life to live

Moving On, Letting Go

When I think about my ex-husband I become enraged
It's suffocating, I feel trapped in a cage
I want to scream so loud, I fear I'll explode
So I squeeze it inside, and I implode
How can one person hurt someone so bad
For twenty-seven years, he's the reason I'm sad
I cry and cry until I'm out of tears
Then I die inside thinking how he's hurt me through the years
There is no love that I have for this man
The image of his face I cannot stand
I hate him are the words I'm afraid to say
So I push it down for it to resurface another day
The only problem, we've been divorced for nine years
And I still blink back the sting of tears
I'm stuck in this circle that goes 'round and 'round
There is no new life for me that I've found
Even in this poem I'm afraid of the rage I'm pushing down
I squeeze my first, tighten my lips, and don't make a sound
I'm so afraid to say, "You stupid piece of ——, I hope you burn in
    hell"
Did that hurt your feelings, oh well
What kind of father walks out on his kids
You are a disgusting pig
I gave up everything for you
Did everything you asked me to
I wish I had the guts to say this to your face
But it would be nothing but a waste
In one ear and out the other, you wouldn't hear a word I say
You would do what you do best, turn, and walk away
I guess it's time for me to hate you and move on
Quite playing this poor me broken record song

The truth is my life is better without you here
Without your lying lips calling me dear
Oh, the sound of your voice makes my stomach sick
I want to yell out, shut up, you stupid prick
This poem is step one to me being free
And finally becoming the amazing wonderful me
The me you will never know because you don't have the ability to
    do so
I can finally let the need for your approval go
I'm not who you say I am
I'm who God says I am
You don't get to decide my life
I'm so glad I'm no longer your wife
You brought me pain and tears for years and years but that part of
    my life is over now
And living without you, I've already learned how
Now I have to learn to get your voice out of my head
And listen to what God says about me instead
But don't worry I'll do that too
Because I'm a fighter, I know that's true!

SOMEDAY

I tell myself that someone will love me someday
I spend my days dreaming of the way he will hold me and what he
    will say
It's become so real in my mind
That I don't feel sad all the time
I dream of the day when I'll have more money than I can spend
I imagine what it feels like to help a stranger, help a friend
To never worry about paying a bill
I think about it so much it feels real
I dream of living in a different time and place
I love it so much, it brings a smile to my face
I keep telling myself I will have all these things someday
These are all the things I ask God for when I pray
I tell myself, "Don't lose hope, keep the dream alive"
Because in the cold dark reality that's how I survive
The reality of my life is like a huge slap in the face
It's nothing like a different time or place
My life feels like a deep dark empty hole
Where every day, there's a battle for my soul
Some days the air is so thick I can't breathe
Some days God graciously gives me a reprieve
But every day, there is an emptiness that I feel in me
I never know how threatening it will be
Some days it's a thought that passes through my mind
Other days I'm afraid my dead body they will find
Some days I cry from the pain that rips through my heart
Some days I cry from the death that keeps us apart
Some days I just sit and feel nothing at all
Some days I scream at the darkness as it closes in on its wall
Some nights as I sleep, I'm betrayed by my own dreams
I wake up shaken by how real it seems

Jesus! I cry out his precious name
He wraps his arms around me and keeps me sane
He never leaves me, not even on the darkest of days
And He leads me because my tears blind the way
It's only when I'm with Him that I feel safe and alive
And it's His power that gives me the strength to survive
It's His love that gives me peace of mind
Through hope in Him is where my joy I find
I don't know how long my life will be this way
But Jesus promises it will be different, someday

FEAR

I can feel fear as it reaches out its hand and wraps it around my throat
It's squeezing tighter, I can't breathe, gasping for air I choke
He's laughing as he sees the terror in my eyes
He has no mercy, he doesn't care about my cries
This disgusting demon is like vapors of black smoke you can't touch
So how can he grip my throat and squeeze so much
He just sneaks in and circles around my feet
He slides up my legs keeping himself nice and neat
I don't even see him until he jumps in my face
I scream and try to run to another place
But he's wrapped around my leg so I fall
With his hands around my neck, I know who to call
"Jesus, help!" Are the words I yell
The terrified demon lets go and runs back to hell
Now who's laughing, this victory was won
By Jesus, God's one and only Son!

BECAUSE OF YOU

Because You first loved me, Your power and grace do I see
Because Your love is special and true, My eyes have been opened to
      see the real You
Because of Your love my life has been spared
You sent Your Son and my burdens He did bear
Your love is a treasure I hold in my heart
A place that forever You will be apart
Your love is my comfort in times of sorrow
So many nights Your shoulder I did borrow
Your love is what gives me the ability
To freely love others as You love me
Your love is the joy that is seen on my face
And I'll share it as I travel from place to place
Your love is the deep passion and desire
That burns in the depths of my soul like a fire
Your love is the emotion that stirs within me
Like the waves tossed about in the sea
Your love is the peace that quiets my mind
Because so often torment I find
Your love is the strength that holds me when I'm weak
You are my rock who daily I will seek
Your love has no beginning or end
Forever, my Lord, I'll call You friend
What can one do to obtain this love
"Nothing," You say, "it's what I'm made of
The love that I have for you is so great
But you will never fully know it until I meet you at My gate
Just know no matter what comes your way
My love is available to you every day
My love for you is what guides My hand
From the beginning before time began"

THANK YOU, FATHER

The end has come, and I'm standing in front of the cross
I have lived a sinful dirty life, and my soul was lost
You sent Your Son to die for me
So we could be together for eternity
I can't imagine the pain You felt
As You watch Your Son being whipped with that belt
His back ripped open as He was being hit again and again
When He did nothing, He committed no sin
The tears that must have streamed down Your face
As Your Son was forced to carry His cross to that place
Did Your stomach grow weak as You watched the nails being driven in
As they pounded them through His flesh again and again
The wrath and anger You must have felt
There were very few people who on their knees they fell
Does the crying and screaming of Your Son still echo in Your mind
Or is there peace You've been able to find
There are no words that I could ever say
To make that tragedy ever seem okay
But what keeps going over and over in my mind
Was that You could have stopped it anytime
You could have said, "I can't take this anymore"
Or these ungrateful people are who we're doing this for
But You didn't, not for a moment or for a blink of an eye
You said You loved me as You watched Your Son die
There are no words to say how overwhelmed I feel
My brain cannot believe this is real
I get to stand before You white as snow
I know from my actions, hell is where I should go
But the love You have for me runs so deep
That You were willing to watch Your Son die while You weep
"Thank You" sounds so empty as it rolls off my tongue
And there is no way to pay You back for giving up Your Son

But I know in my heart this much is true
I will shout to the world how much I love You
I will always tell of Your amazing grace
And about what You suffered so I could see Your face
You're the King of kings, the Great I Am
There is no power that in front of You could stand
You're my Abba, my Father, my very best Friend
And I will praise You until forever has an end

REVELATION

Revelation…the word itself is full of such fear
Butterflies in my stomach, the time of judgment is near
My legs grow weak as I think about all I've done
My sins are so great, I could never count every one
I see Satan and his demons as they fall into the bottomless pit
Screaming, crying, and throwing a fit
There are multitudes of angels singing above
Of God's power, His glory, and His love
My time has come to stand before God
But I can't, I fall to my knees and sob
He has His book, and He finds my name
Why are you crying? You know why My Son came
When I look at you, I don't see what you've done
I only see the blood of My precious Son
Why do you cry? Your salvation is complete
It is Satan and his followers who meet their defeat
My precious child, you've wasted much of your life
Living in fear, giving into daily strife
You've heard Me speak these words, "You're free"
That doesn't just apply to eternity
When you wake up in the morning and go to bed at night
You never had to worry, you never had to fight
I was there with My arms open wide
I was your safety, your place to hide
Your story's not over, the end is not here
Come to Me, and let Me dry up your tears
You know the beauty of what's up ahead
The streets of gold, the bride I wed
That's a promise that can never be lost
My Son has already paid the cost
It's your life that you're living now that matters most
You're My child, and that's where I want to boast

Give yourself to Me everyday
Take My hand, I'll lead the way
The life I have planned out for you
Is full of joy, peace, and love too
Don't worry about this world or how you will fit in
I was with you in the beginning, and I will be with you till the end
My love for you is greater than you'll ever know
I gave up what was most precious to me to make you white as snow
There is nothing in your life that's not in My control
So don't get run down, and let life take its toll
You may not understand all my ways
But all I need is your trust each and every day
Follow the path that I've laid out ahead
And don't get lost overthinking things in your head
Life is simple when your eyes are on Me
So smile, shout, rejoice because you're free
Go spread the word, I want everyone to know
Through My Son, you're white as snow…

ONE DAY AT A TIME

I'm slipping, Lord, please grab my hand
My legs are weak, and I can no longer stand
I feel so wretched all through my soul
And my mind is spinning out of control
I don't want to feel what's building up inside
But where can I go? Where can I run?
I can't hide in the dark, and I can't hide in the sun
It's not You, Lord, that causes my heart to break
It's my life and the people who cause such pain
I feel like I'm always walking in the rain
I see sunshine on the other side of the street
But the rain follows the direction of my feet
No matter where I go, no matter what I do
I can't find Your joy that's true
I eat, I shop, I get lost in the TV
But everything leaves me feeling empty
I study Your word and sing Your praise
But my heart is still sad and my mind a daze
My life is empty because I'm all alone
With the exception of my two boys at home
I don't trust anyone, I know I'm going to get hurt
I'm just sick and tired of being treated like dirt
I'm a person, and my feelings matter
And I'm not going to sit here and get fatter and fatter
I'm sick of being the victim, I can't do it anymore
But how do I not be without needing to settle a score
How do I let go when the pain is so deep
How do I get to the other side when the hill is so steep
How can I be who You want me to be
So I can let go of the past and be free
The desire of my heart is to please You, Lord
And with You and Your Word, I am never bored

I feel like a failure in Your sight
I just feel like I never get it right
Heal my wounds, but leave the scars
So I can show the world how amazing You are
Help me, Lord, to make a fresh start
Where I wake up every day, and You fill my heart
Help me, Lord, to take care of myself
And stop shoving my feelings on a shelf
We will take things one day at a time
And You can slowly break my chains that bind
Thank You for listening and always being here
In my weakness, You always draw me near
I love You so much, I hope You know
Especially when my actions don't say so
I feel so much better, I have the strength to go on
Every day I will sing Your praises in my song

RUNNING TO YOU

I run from this pencil lead
Because of the tears I don't want to shed
The pain I feel is deep in my soul
And by running I feel like I've gained control
How foolish am I to think this way
To think I have power to control any day
If running is something I must do
Then I'm running straight to You
The healing I feel in Your embrace
And the love that fills me because of Your grace
Is what I need most right now
So at Your feet, I humbly bow
Take this emptiness that I offer You
And fill it with whatever You want to
My desires, my hopes, and my dreams
Are the very thing that makes me scream
Scream and cry and stamp my feet
My tantrums praise has a repetitive beat
The words are the same every time
I want, I want, I want what's mine
So I embrace Your will for me
I won't run from who You need me to be
My god is no longer my broken heart
You have all of me, each and every part
I love You, Lord, more and more every day
I'll hold Your hand, and You lead the way

It Was Always You

All my life I've searched for ways to be filled and satisfied
But I never found it, no matter how hard I tried
I tried to find it by having a man
You know, filled with love, walking hand in hand
I thought I'd have it with all my money
But all that showed me is that people are scummy
Boy, how they love you when you're flush with cash
They have no problem helping to spend your stash
I bought things, I ate things, but I was empty
I broke down, full of self-pity
When my legs were closed, and my money was gone
And in my broken heart was not one song
I wiped the tears from my eyes and looked around
There was not one friend to be found
I felt so broken and lonely, and the tears would not stop
I thought all this could be over with one pop
Pop of the pills, pop of a gun
Who would care, from this world I was shunned
But in my weakest moment, my darkest hour
I felt this hand and was captivated by its power
I reached out and grabbed the hand
Through its power and might, I was able to stand
I could feel His gentle touch wipe the tears from my eyes
And His arms embraced me and soothed all my cries
I began to feel something I never felt before
And I could feel healing in all the places that tore
The thoughts in my mind began to change
And this feeling in me was so strange
It's something I've never felt before
But it was everything I've spent my life looking for
I feel full and complete and satisfied
My heart feels full, and I didn't even try

It was you that I've looked for all my life
Everything was made right as I looked in the eyes of Christ
You showed me what true love was when You died on the cross
To be with me, You were willing to pay the cost
You love me, that's what You said the night You died
And You know everything about me, I don't need to hide
You know who I am, You know what I've done
You were with me in my darkest hour, Jesus
You are my bright morning sun
This world has nothing to offer that's meaningful and true
All my life I've searched for something that can only be found in you
Love, joy, peace, and acceptance too
You gave me a family to belong to
The turmoil of this world will always be here
But it can't harm me with You near
You are my strength and my shield
My empty and broken soul to You do I yield
Take it, change it, do whatever You want to
Because, Jesus, it was always You
It was You that I needed when I felt abandoned and alone
It was You that I needed when I was searching for a place to call home
It was always You, I just didn't know it until I looked into Your eyes
That You were the answer to all my cries
I love You with more passion than my words can express
And for the first time in my life, in Your arms, my soul is at rest
Thank You, Jesus, for not leaving me
And for showing me who You want me to be
I pray my life will bring You glory
And I pray that I will bring You honor as I share my story
I know I'm still broken, but that's the best part
You told me, You only care about what's in my heart
And what's in my heart is desire and love or You
And a willingness to do whatever You tell me to
"I trust You completely," those are words I never thought I'd say
And I freely give myself to You every day
Loneliness, fear, and anxiety have a hold on me no more
My chains are broken and with eagle's wings I'll soar

REAL LOVE

The path of one's life is so different but so much the same
We laugh, we love, we feel joy, we feel pain
Sometimes sorrow can run so deep in our souls
And the weight of that over the years can take its toll
Even when I try so hard to break away and be free
There's always a little black cloud following me
Its raindrops are like acid-burning holes in my mind
Whispering little words that are anything but pleasant and kind
They are footholds for Satan's little beast
Filling my thoughts with enough doubt for a feast
He fills my head with the same lie over and over again
I listen to him so much, you would think he's my friend
I turn to You, God, for Your gentle, loving touch
Because my soul thirsts for it so much
I pour out my heart and cry my tears
Like I've done with You for so many years
I ask the same question of You every time
The question that's been forever burned in my mind
Why, God, did You choose me
I can't be the person You thought I'd be
I mess up all the time, I make horrible mistakes
And I know my choices have made Your heart break
But here You are loving me so
Holding me tight, never letting go
You stroke my hair and look into my eyes
And ask me, Why would you believe Satan's lies
I know who you are from beginning to end
And I'm truly your very best friend
I've made no mistake in choosing you
I have very important things for you to do
Perfection is something that I have never asked
It's your own dark shadow that you cast

I have created you exactly the way you are
And together you and I will go so far
The mistakes you make help us grow closer together
And with My Son's blood, I have bought you forever
So don't be afraid if you get it right or wrong
It's My love in your heart that makes you strong
Remember if you fall to land on your knees
Call out to Me, and I will help you with ease
Remember that I love you in a very special way
And I walk beside you every single day
Your chains are broken, and you're free
So be who I created you to be

My Boys

The sorrow in my heart is so heavy I can hardly breathe
It's pulling me down deep, it's dark, I can barely see
I miss you so much, every other weekend when you're gone
But vacations are torture, the days just go on and on
I miss you so much, I just want my boys home
The silence is so loud in this house when I'm alone
I try to be brave, to stand ever so strong
To not show my tears as the years move on
Three years have now passed, and it hardly seems fair
I wasn't the betrayer, but you don't care
You stand so tall like you're so great
Like the hell we live through isn't because of your mistake
I just want to have a normal life
To be a mother, to be a wife
You stole my dream when you betrayed my heart
And our two innocent boys' lives are being ripped apart
I feel so much anger that I'm consumed with hate
But be patient, I just have to wait
For one more day to come and go
Just one more day, and they will be home

TORMENT

I can hear you laughing in the lonely silence I hear
Your bitter, cold words in the drop of every tear
You relentless demon, just let me be
The haunting image of your face is all I see
You dip your finger and twist things around in my mind
The smile on your face as my chains you bind
Falling deeper and deeper I just close my eyes
And for a moment it seems as if I believe your lies
I truly wonder what's so good about me
And what possible reason for my life could there be
I'm always the one who's looking at life from the outside
I'm always the one who wants to run and hide
You're no good, you're ugly, you're fat, and you're stupid too
Why on earth would anyone want to be around you
You've told me these lies since I was a girl
In my mind, they float, swim, and swirl
God tells me these things are not true
And I want to believe Him, more than anything I do
I want to wake up every day and feel His joy and peace
But the torment from these demons just won't cease
I know You're stronger, Lord, than any demon can be
But as I turn from him, he digs his claws deeper into me
The pain I feel hurts so bad
That I just sit crying, feeling sad
If I would just stop fighting You, I know You could pull me away
And save me from the hell I live in every day
I know my wounds You could heal with Your love
And You can tell my heart all the precious things You made me of
Help me, Lord, not to live in fear
The whisper of Your voice I pray I will hear
I love You, Lord, that's one thing that's true
My soul was created to praise and honor You

I can see more clearly all of Satan's lies
He will never have me, no matter how hard he tries
I know no matter what happens You will never leave my side
And I know from You I can never run and hide
I know the love You have for me runs deep
Your Son dying on the cross is the image in my mind I will keep
It's all I need to truly be free ·
The battle was already won the moment He died for me!

MY DREAM

As I look up at the moon in the night sky
I can't help but wonder what significance am I
I feel so lost in Your great story
I want my life to bring You glory
But I haven't done anything in my life so far
That would say to anyone this is who You are
Yes, I've written a few poems from time to time
But they are special, something I claim as mine
I'm afraid all the time to do what I want to
I want to let go and give myself to You
To trust You and love You and finally be free
To walk with boldness and just be me
To have a thought or opinion to claim as mine
To let my gifts and talents shine
Not to care what other people say
Not to give in to their way
They broke my spirit and crushed me down
So I walled myself in so no one's around
But being alone isn't my dream
It just makes me cry and scream
It makes me feel angry and hate inside
And every day a little more of me dies
I must step out of the darkness and into the light
And stop relying on me and start walking in Your might
All I know is I love You, so I give my dream to You.

ALREADY FREE

All I want is to love You, Lord
But my heart is pierced with Satan's sword
It seems no matter how hard I try
I can't get past these tears I cry
The blackness of this hole I keep falling in
It has no beginning, and it has no end
I wake up each day and long to die
To finally have peace and not struggle to just get by
How long, Lord, till can finally be free
Until You unlock these chains that bind me
Have mercy on me just for today
Make this torture stop and go away
What, Lord, what did You say
You unlocked my chains the other day
Then I must be tangled because I didn't know
That You gave me the power and freedom to go
"I'm not tangled," is that what You said
Then my legs must be broken instead
Heal my legs so I can get up and walk
And run from Satan, that sly little fox
What it's not true, how can this be
My legs are fine… I see
It must be the darkness because I didn't know
That this whole time I could go
What, Lord, I can't hear You through my cries
Oh, I see, just open my eyes
Why am I here, what reason could there be
What, Lord, it's because of me
I'm the reason I feel this way
Is that right, Lord, is that what You say
Well, I guess there's only one thing left to do
Get the heck out of this place and start serving You

SAFE IN HEAVEN

My precious daughter, please don't cry
Your daddy is safe here by My side
I know you miss him, and the pain runs deep
And you think your eyes will do nothing but weep
But never forget that I'm by your side
And from Me, My child, you need not hide
I will give you all the strength you need
When you feel all you can do is fall to your knees
Just rest your head on My chest
And I will take care of the rest
Your dad now sees you through my eyes
And never again will he feel pain or cry
He has seen your life from beginning to end
And he's so proud of you, you should see his grin
Your dad will be with you in whatever you do
Because he has joined the angels that walk with you
So close your eyes and feel My arm's loving embrace
And allow Me to dry the tears from your face
We'll get through it together hand in hand
As you make your footprints in the sand

I'M SORRY

I'm sorry, Lord, I have failed again
When will this torment end
I'm so lonely that my soul aches
And I do things that make Your heart break
I'm just so tired of being alone
I want a man there when I come home
But instead, I've traded my soul for ten minutes of sex
And I'm afraid of what I will do next
All I've ever wanted was for someone to love me
But no matter what it just can't be
I don't understand why it's so hard to find
Or why Satan chooses this to torment my mind
Help me, Lord, that's my plea
And no matter what I do, don't turn Your eye from me
My desire is to be good, but my flesh is weak
Making You smile is the joy I seek
I'm sorry I fail time and time again
I can't say it will ever end
I just need a husband to make things right
So I can be pure in Your sight
Choose one for me because my picks are no good
And send him to me soon if You would
I love You, Lord, and I will not turn away
And I will try to please You every day
Thank You for Your grace on the days I don't
Those are the days I need You most
I love You, Lord, and I give You my heart to mend
Thank You for Your forgiveness… Amen

ON EAGLE'S WINGS

I woke up today and dropped to my knees
Finding myself with the same worn-out pleas
The calculations that go around and around in my mind
Are taking up all the spaces where I would normally find
The stress is so madding and the anxiety so high
I cannot wait for this moment of my life to go by
I wake up today, and I'm on my knees again
Only this story has a different end
I close my eyes, and I can feel Your grace
As each burden is lifted, I float into space
A space where this world, and all its cares
Is a place where I'm free form the burden it bears
I'm free to feel the might of Your hand
Gently guiding me where You want me to stand
I'm free to hear the soft words You speak
And it's Your wisdom I truly seek
I can feel Your breath breathing life into me
And through Your eyes is how I want to see
Everything about You is perfect my Lord
In this prayer on eagle's wings, I soared
You never leave me, and You give me all I need
But sometimes, I get blinded by this world's greed
Forgive me, Lord, and let those times be few
Thank You for letting them remind me how much I love You
You, my Lord, are the love of my life
I am your bride… Your faithful wife
This love we share has no end
You are truly my very best friend
Always and forever my heart belongs to You
I will praise You in whatever You call me to do
So in those moments when chaos fills my mind
And the torment of anxiety is the chains that bind

Send Your Spirit to sing over me
So I will remember to get down on my knees
And fly to the place where I can truly be free
Where Your peace and mercy flow into me

ABOUT THE AUTHOR

Kris is a single mom of two boys, and she lives in Southern California. She loves Jesus, and He has been her strength throughout her life. She has been writing poetry since she was a teenager, and it is the only way that she knows how to express her true feelings.